CLASSIC PIANO REPERTOIRE
WILLIAM GILLOCK

12 EXQUISITE PIANO SOLOS

T0071690

ISBN 978-1-4584-0553-1

WILLIS MUSIC

EXCLUSIVELY DISTRIBUTED BY

HAL•LEONARD® CORPORATION

7777 W. BLUEMOUND RD. P.O. BOX 13819 MILWAUKEE, WI 53213

Visit Hal Leonard Online at
www.halleonard.com

"**WILLIAM GILLOCK** is one of a select group of composers for piano teaching whose works are almost invariably successful as music, and also successful where it counts equally, with the students. The Gillock name spells magic to teachers around the world... In each Gillock composition, no matter what the teaching purpose, musical quality comes first."

— Lynn Freeman Olson, renowned pianist and pedagogue
Clavier magazine, February 1979

WILLIAM GILLOCK (1917-1993), noted music educator and composer, was born in LaRussell, Missouri, where he learned to play the piano at an early age. After graduating from Central Methodist College, his musical career led him to long tenures in New Orleans and Dallas, where he was in high demand as a teacher, clinician, and composer. He was also known as the "Schubert of children's composers" in tribute to his extraordinary melodic gift, and published numerous piano solos and ensembles for students of all levels. William Gillock was honored on multiple occasions by the *National Federation of Music Clubs* (NFMC) with the Award of Merit for Service to American Music, and his music remains remarkably popular throughout the United States and throughout the world.

FROM THE PUBLISHERS

The *Classic Piano Repertoire* series includes popular as well as lesser-known pieces from a select group of composers out of the Willis piano archives (established in 1899). This volume features 12 piano solos by William Gillock; each one carefully selected, each one a true miniature gem. The music has been newly engraved and edited with the aim to preserve Gillock's original intent and musical purpose.

CONTENTS

To Tommy Eaton

Festive Piece

William Gillock

Con moto ($\bowtie$ = ca. 104)

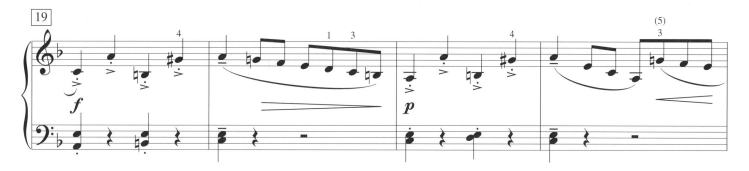

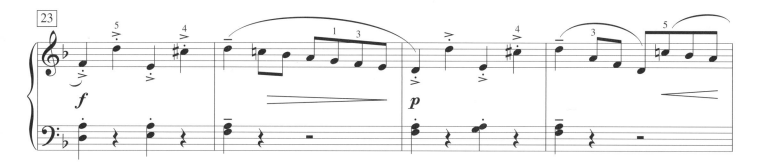

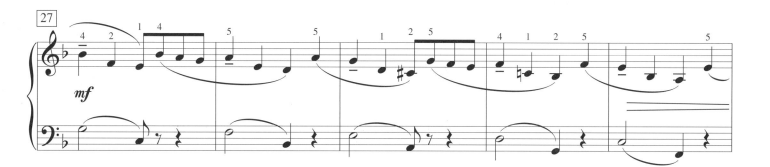

Sunset

William Gillock

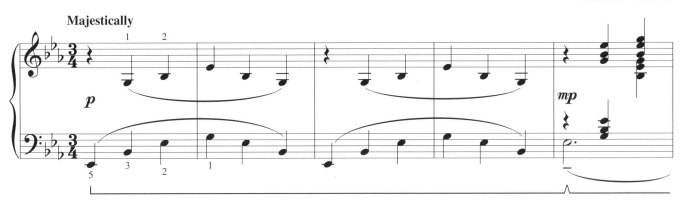

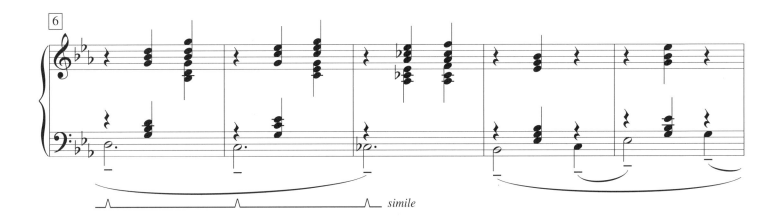

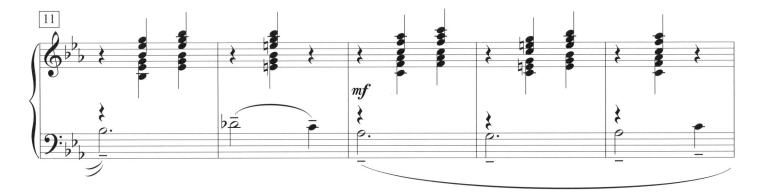

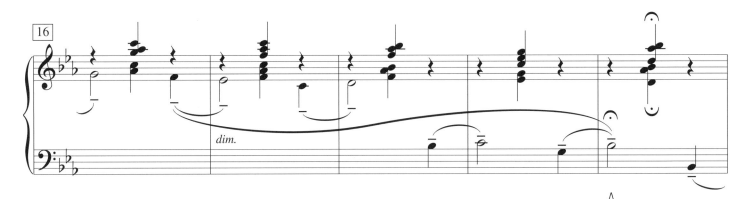

* Both hands *8va* on half notes.

Etude in G Major
(Toboggan Ride)

William Gillock

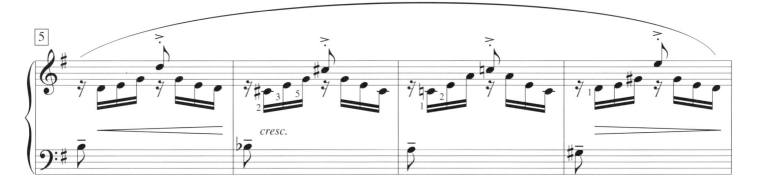

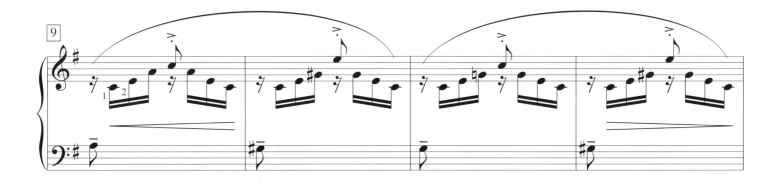

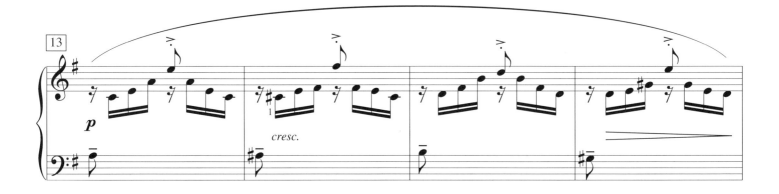

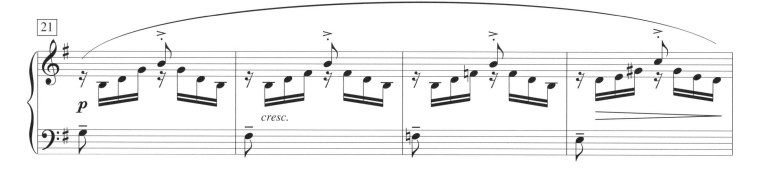

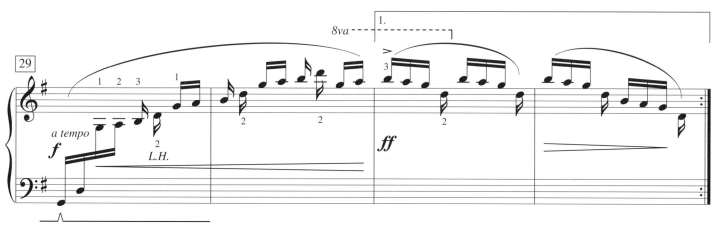

To the Hawai'i chapter of the National Guild of Piano Teachers

Polynesian Nocturne

William Gillock

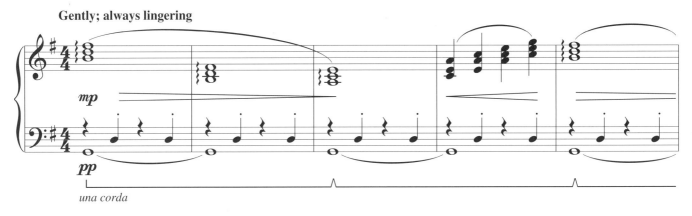

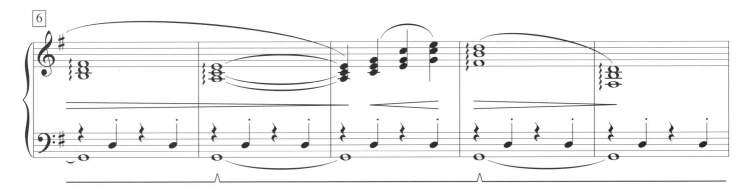

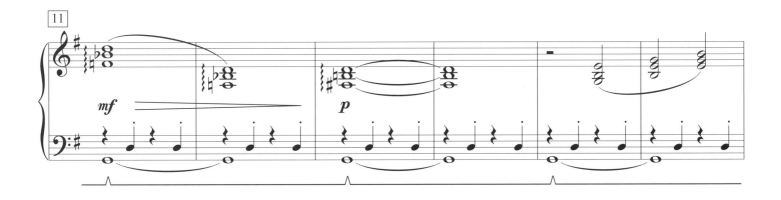

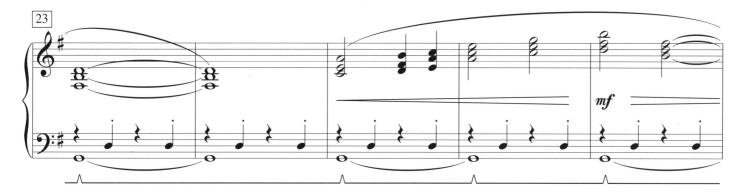

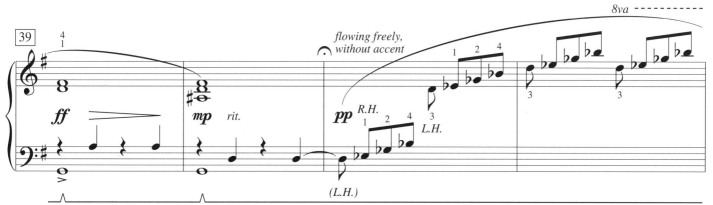

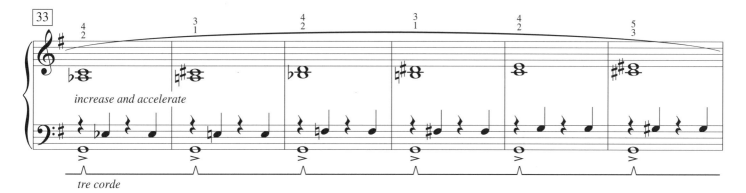

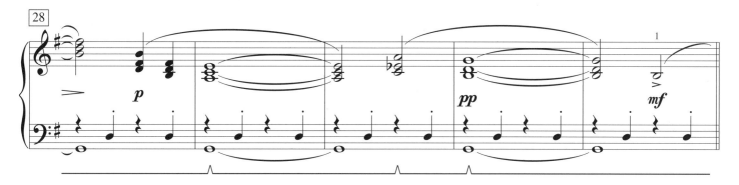

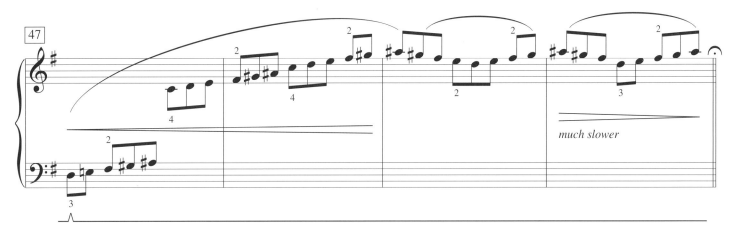

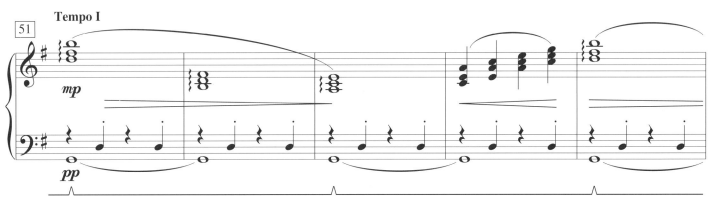

Tempo I

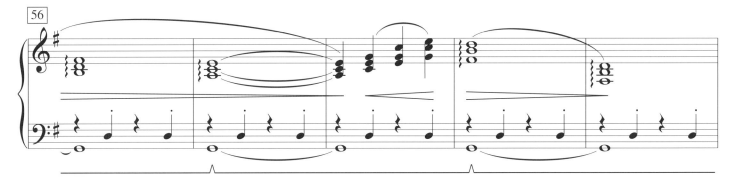

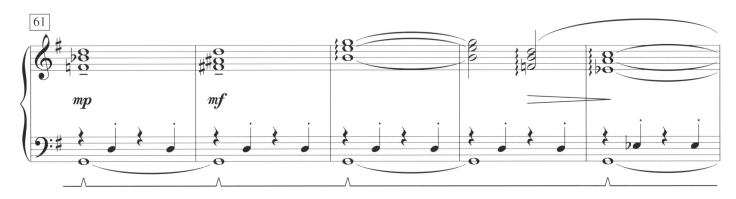

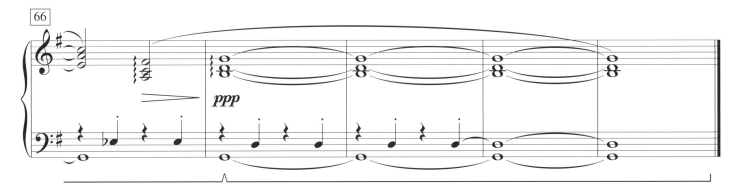

To Naomi Singleton

Classic Carnival
"Programmatic Sonatina"

I. ROYAL CONCERT

William Gillock

Con poco moto (𝅝 = ca. 92)

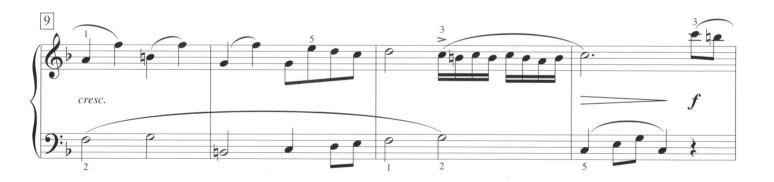

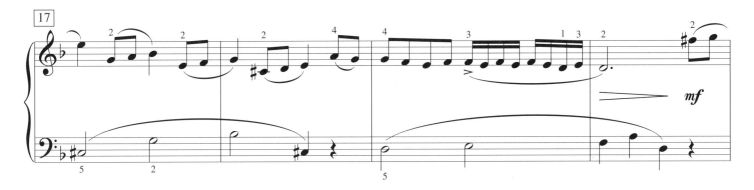

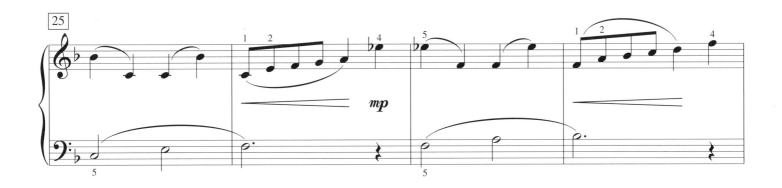

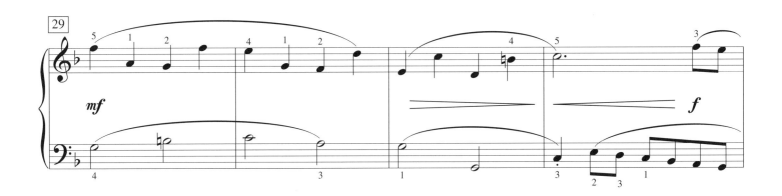

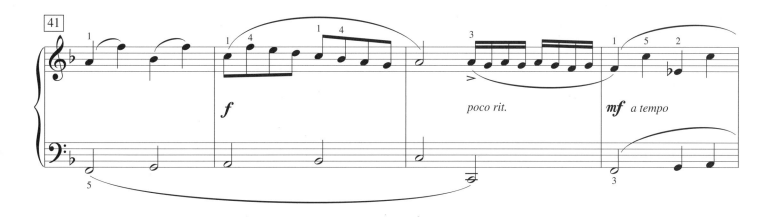

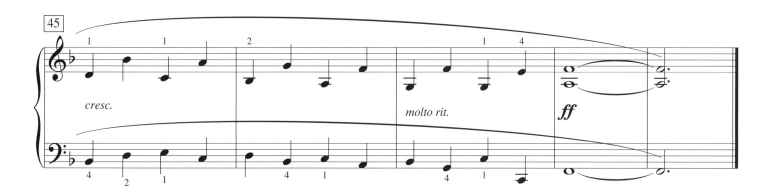

II. RELIGIOUS PROCESSION

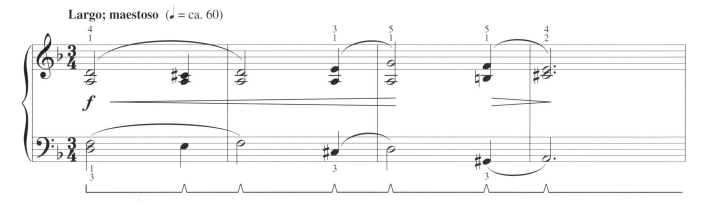

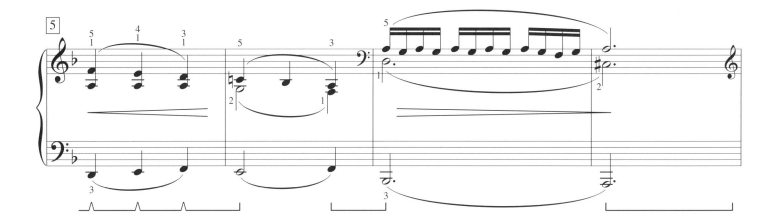

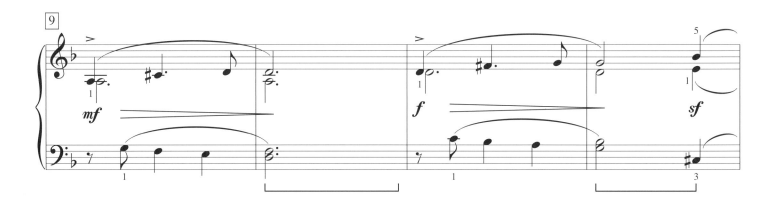

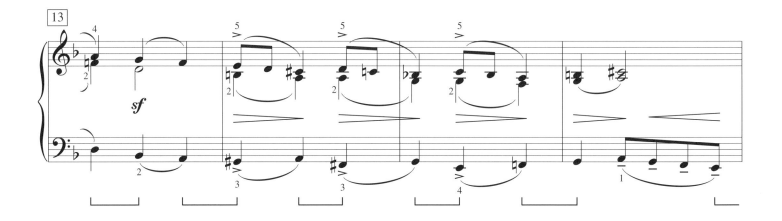

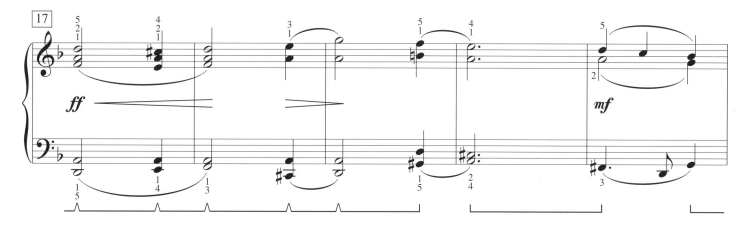

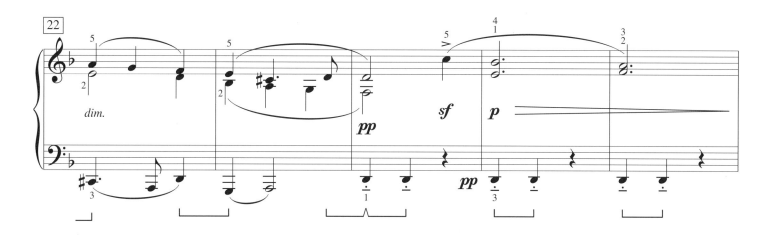

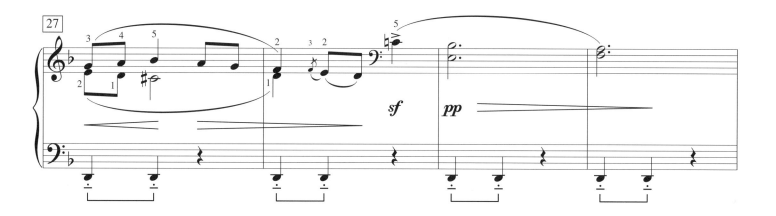

III. CARNIVAL BALL

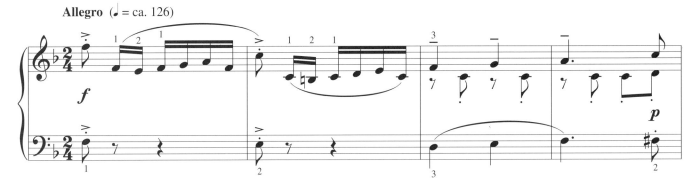

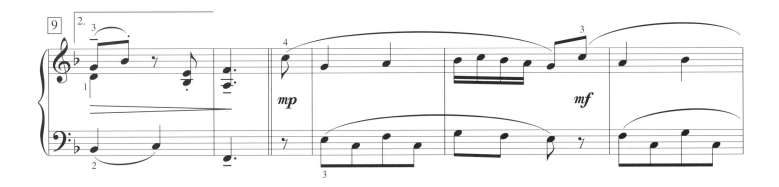

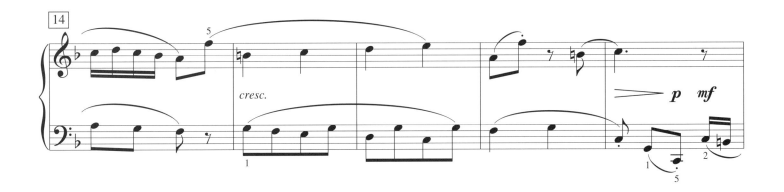

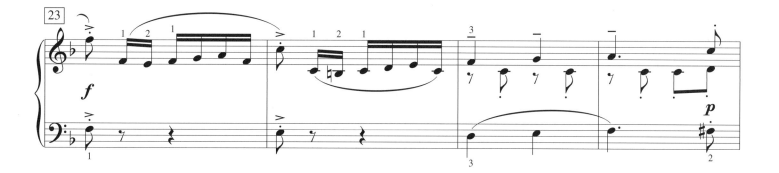

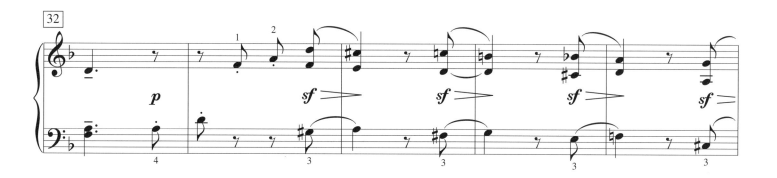

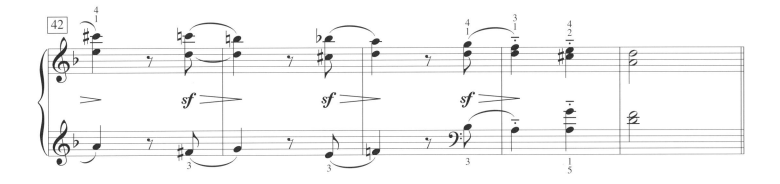

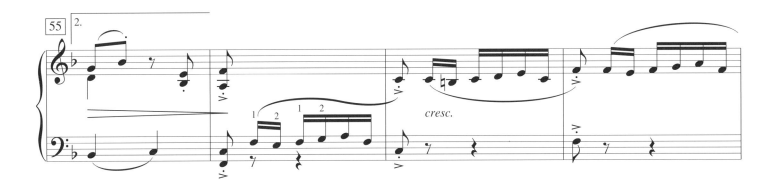

* Strike grace note and following note simultaneously.

To my friend, Ralph Jusko

Etude in E Minor

William Gillock

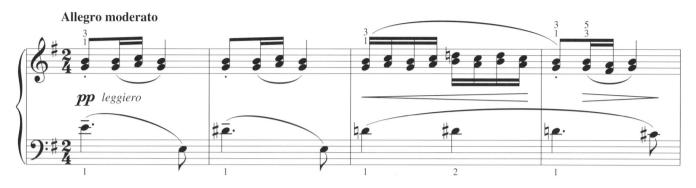

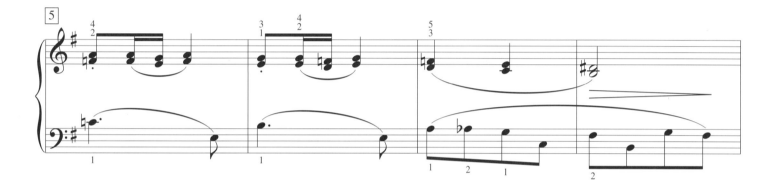

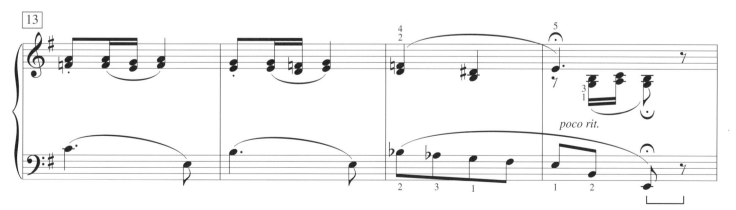

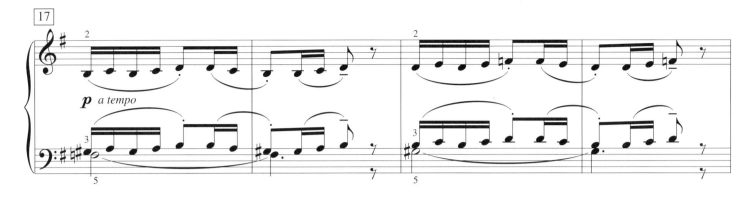

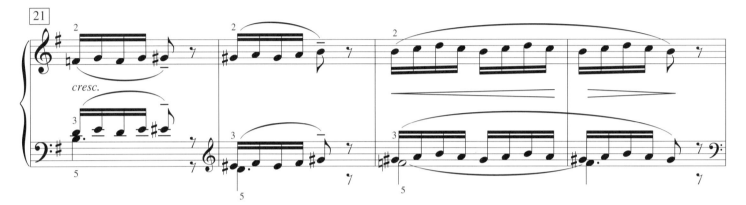

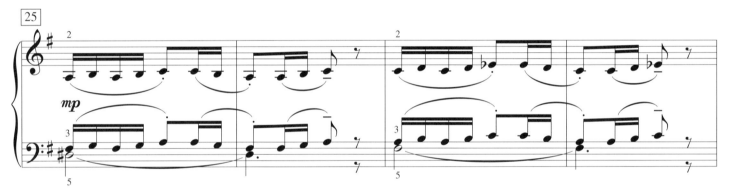

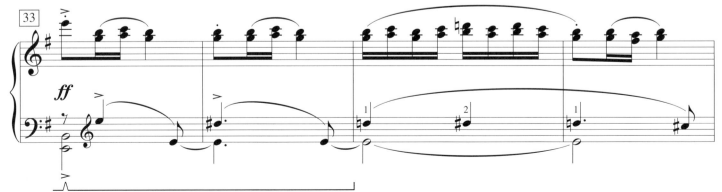

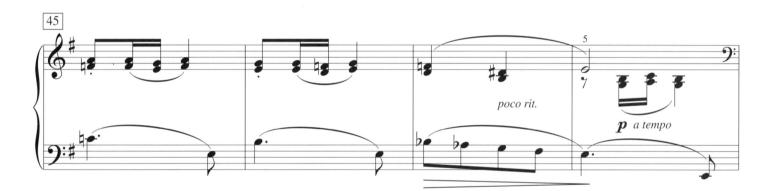

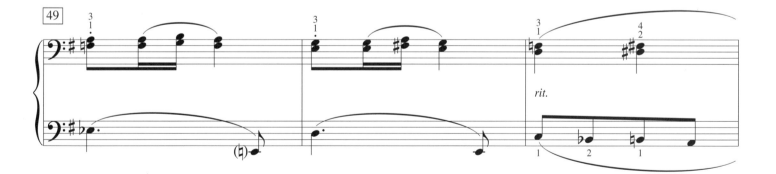

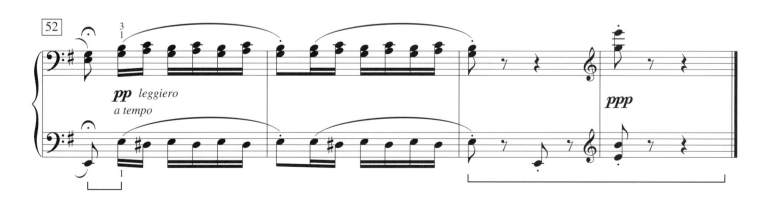

To Robert Harris

Nocturne

William Gillock

Very quietly; lingering (♩ = ca. 58)

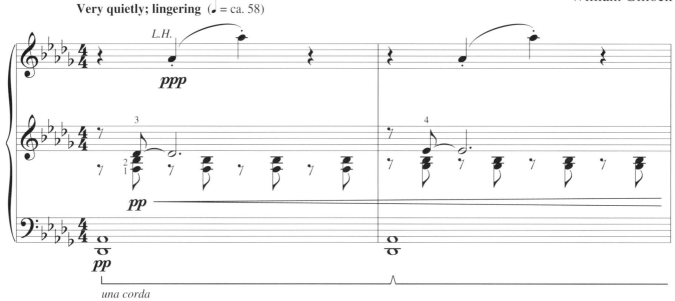

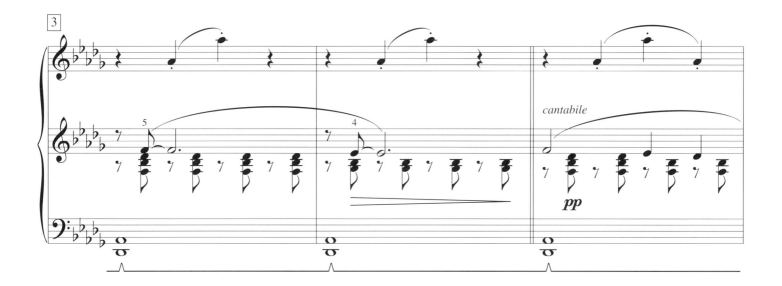

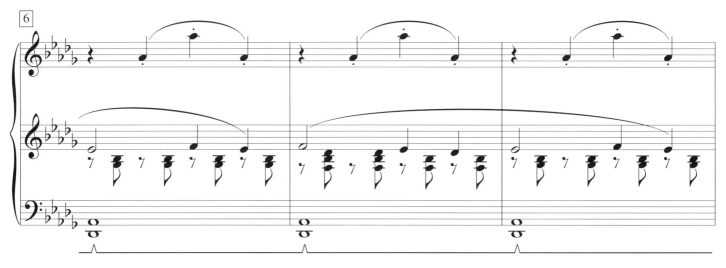

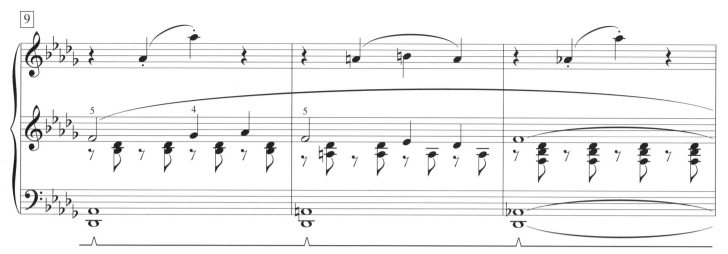

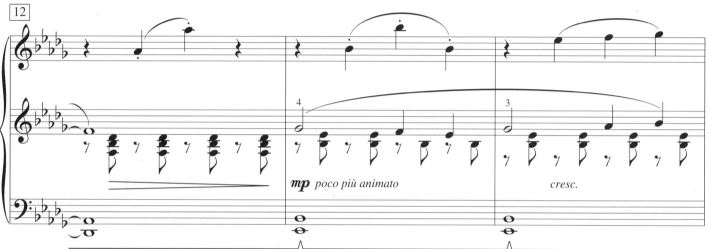

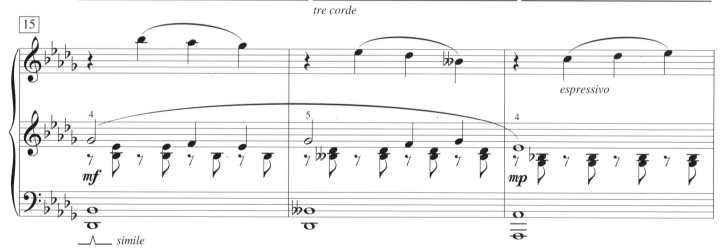

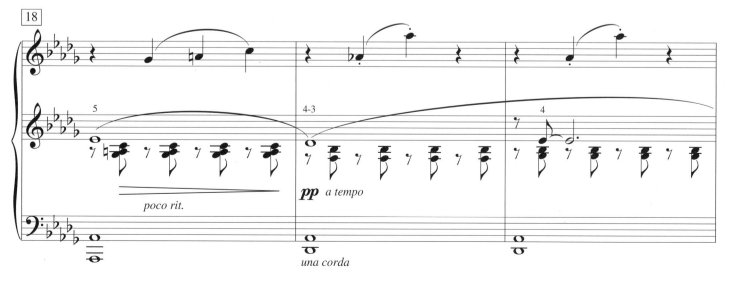

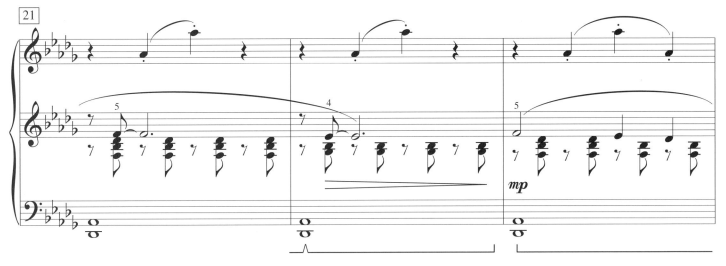

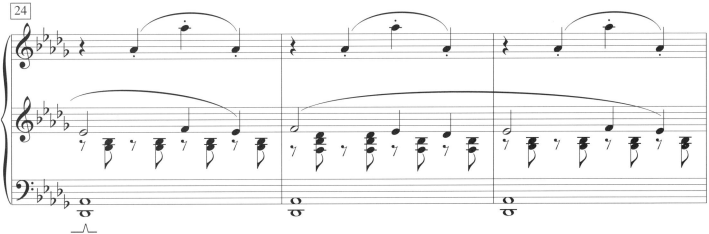

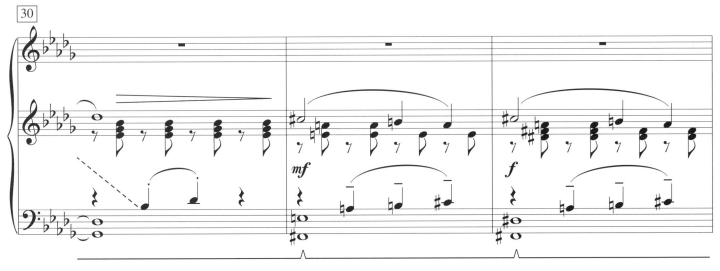

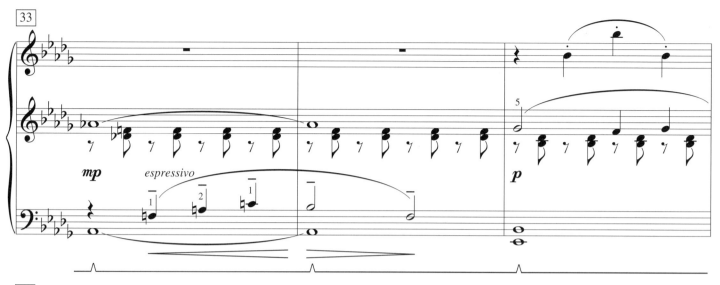

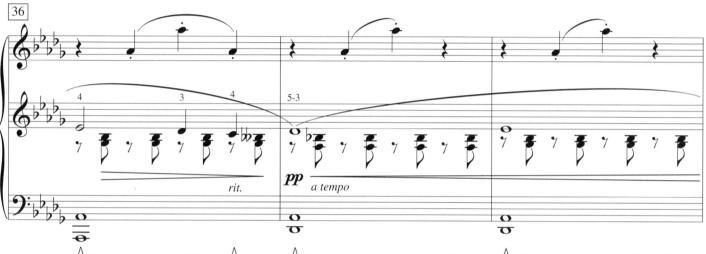

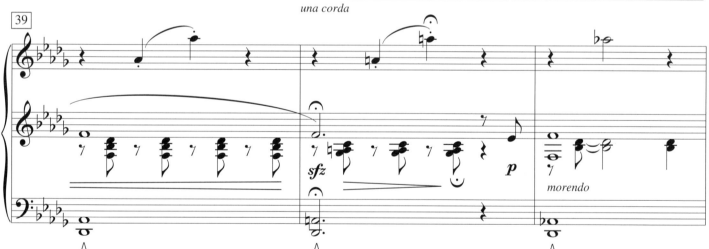

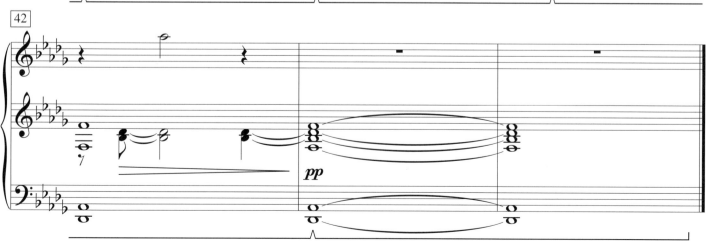

To Ruby Simons Vought

Sonatina in Classic Style

William Gillock

Allegro deciso

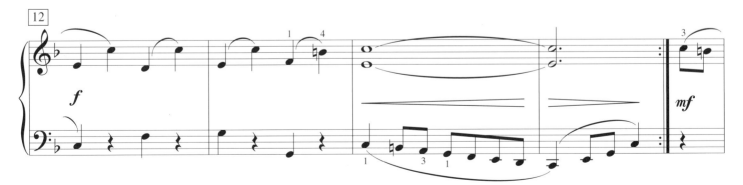

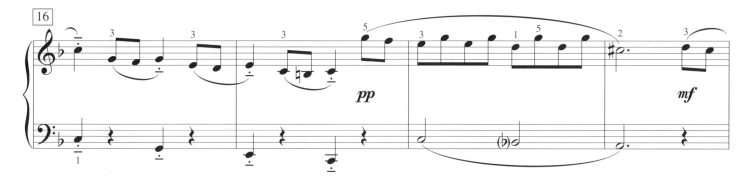

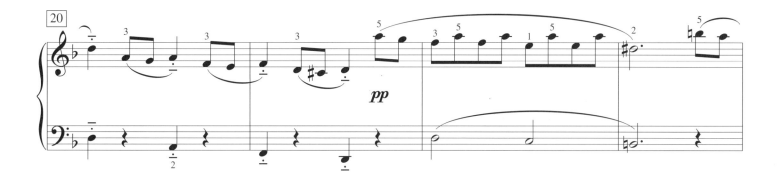

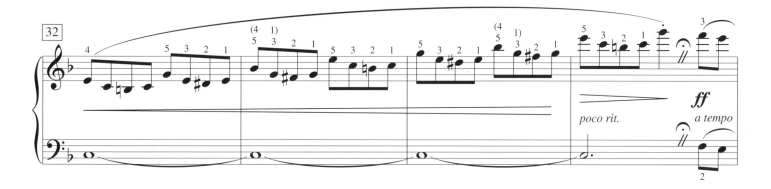

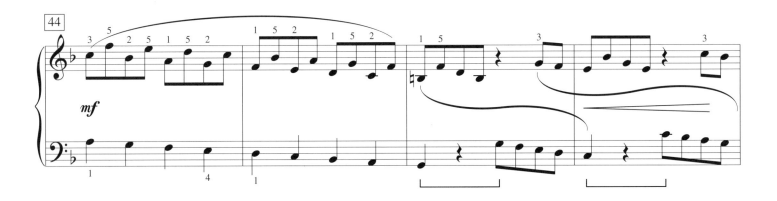

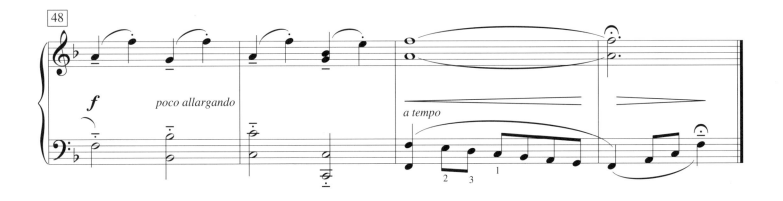

Andante con espressione

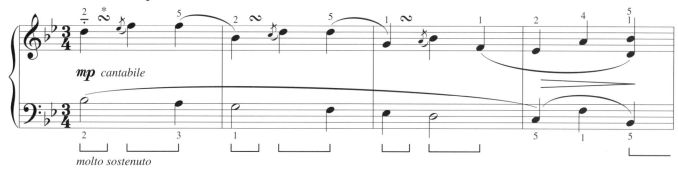

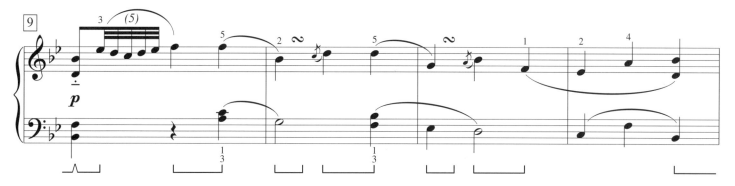

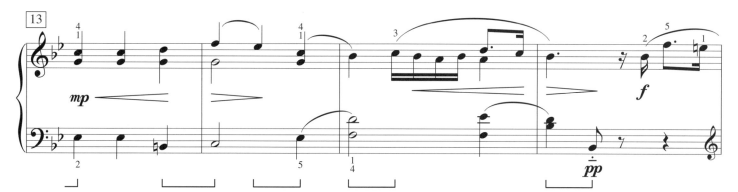

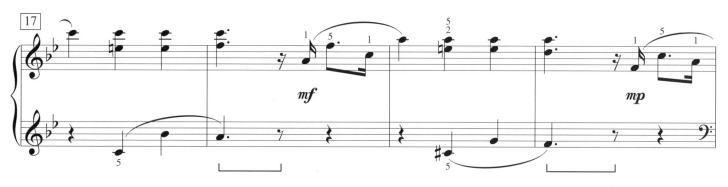

* In the 1959 publication, the turn is written out as an implied quintuplet throughout the movement:

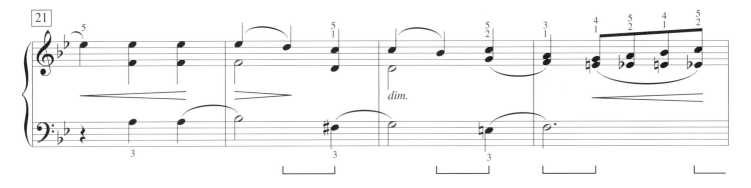

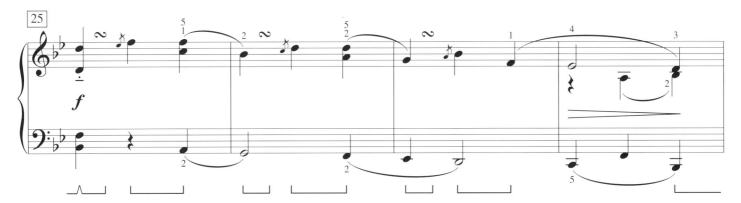

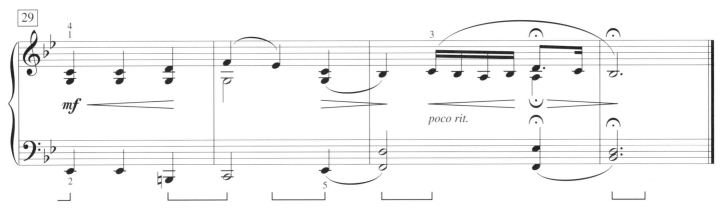

Rondo: Allegro vivace

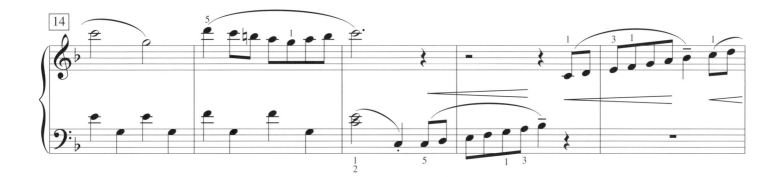

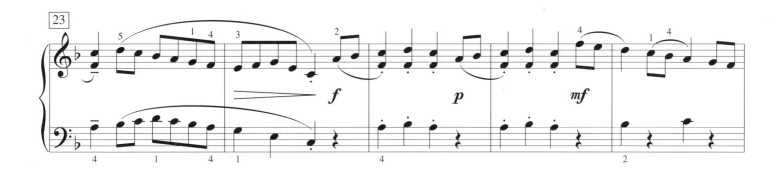

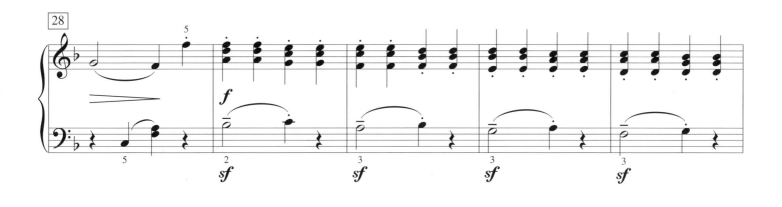

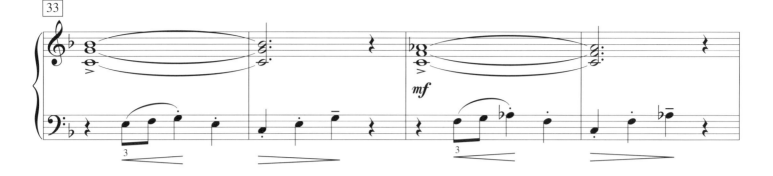

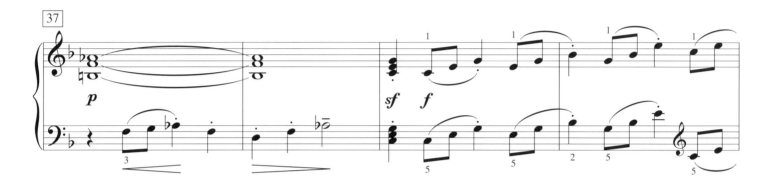

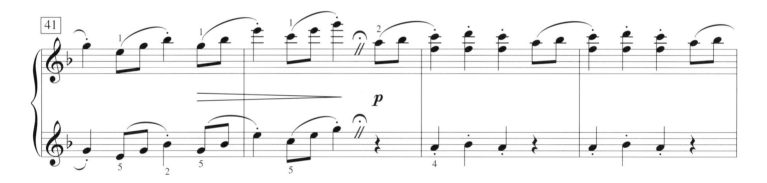

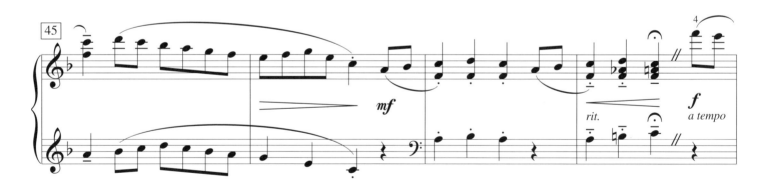

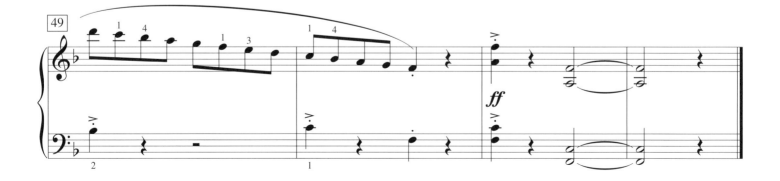

Dedicated to Tompkins County Junior Music Clubs, Ithaca, New York

Etude in A Major
(The Coral Sea)

William Gillock

Gently rolling (♩ = ca. 112)

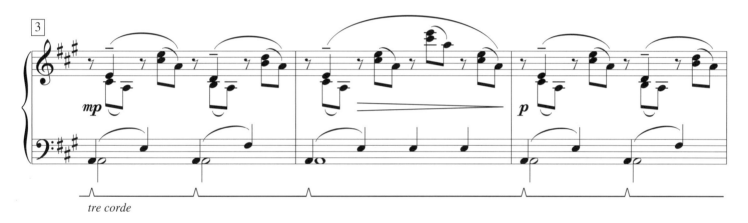

Poco più mosso (♩ = ca. 126)

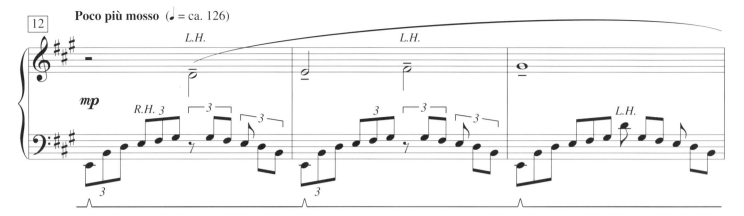

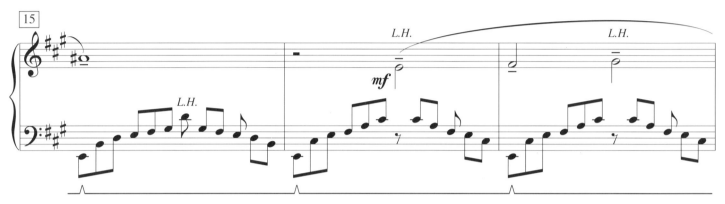

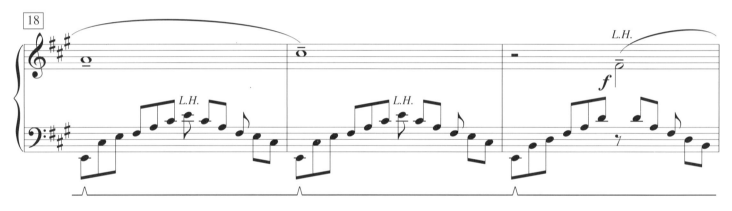

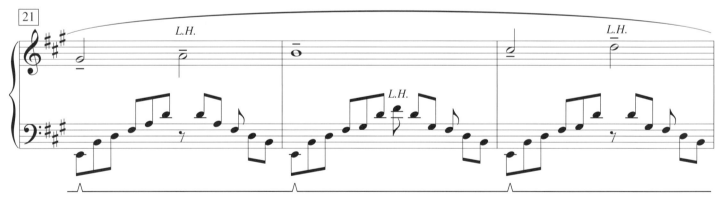

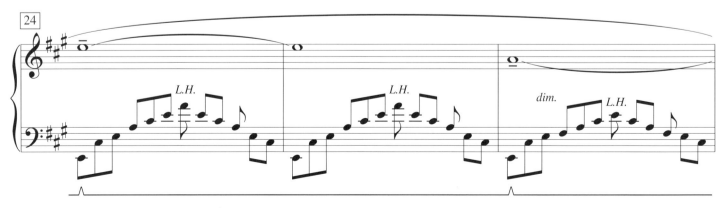

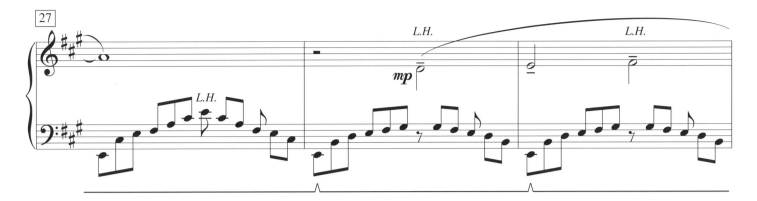

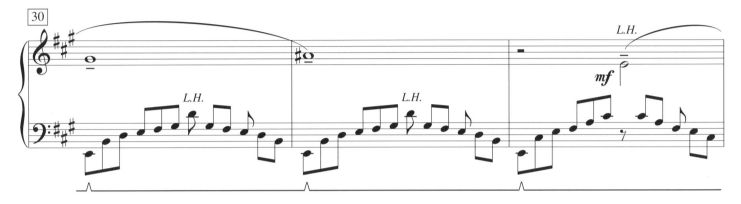

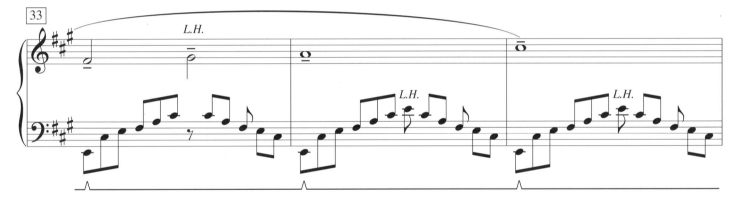

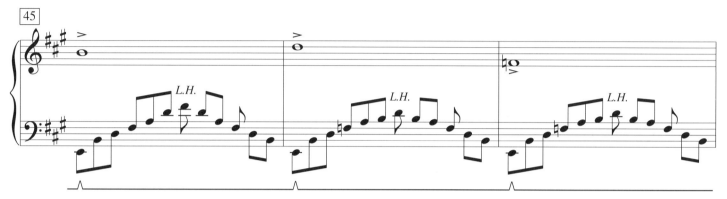

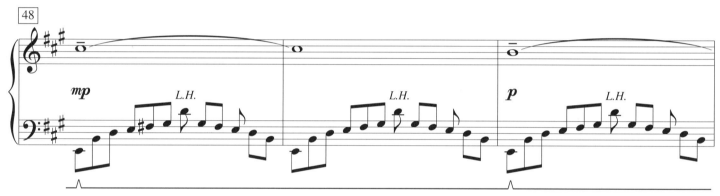

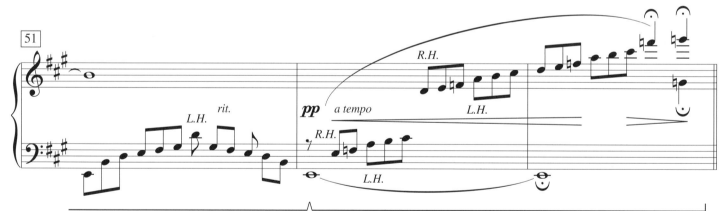

una corda

Tempo I

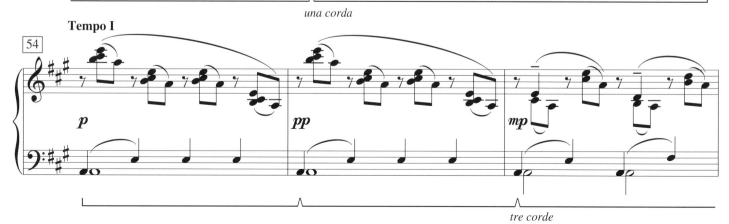

tre corde

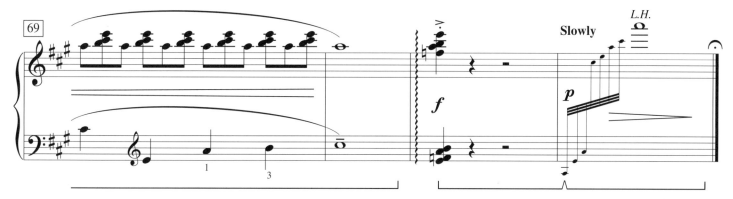

To Eugenia O'Reilly

A Memory of Vienna

William Gillock

Tempo di valse lento, con molto rubato

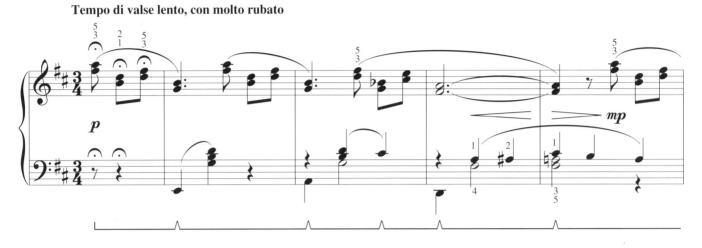

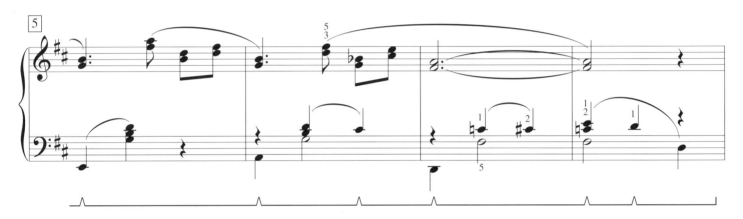

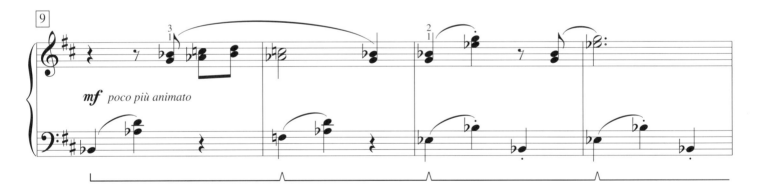

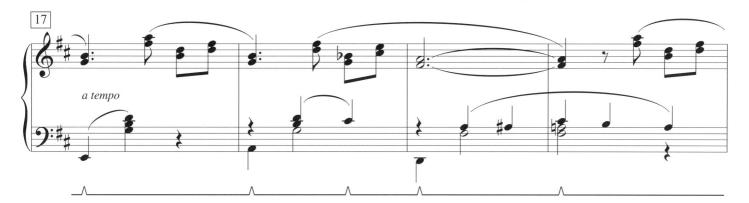

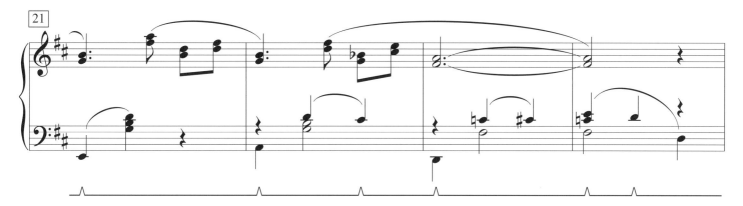

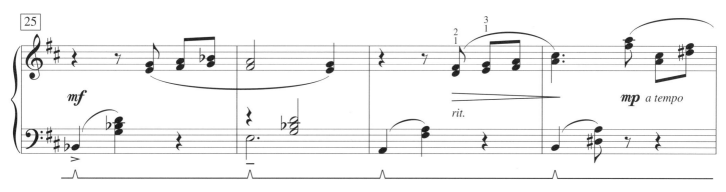

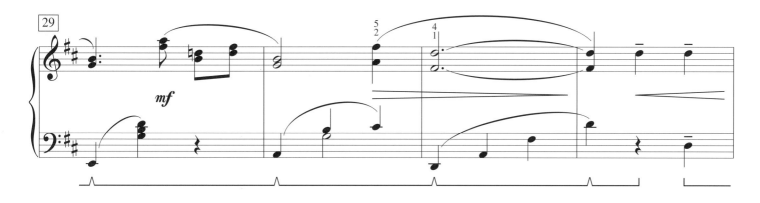

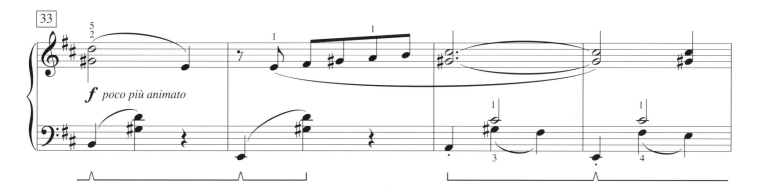

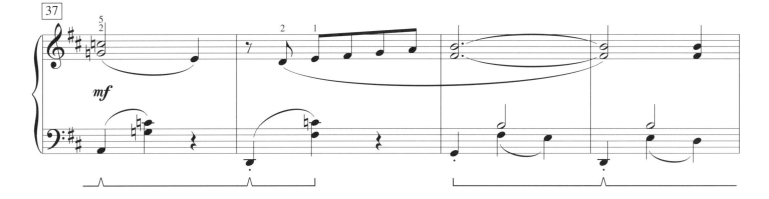

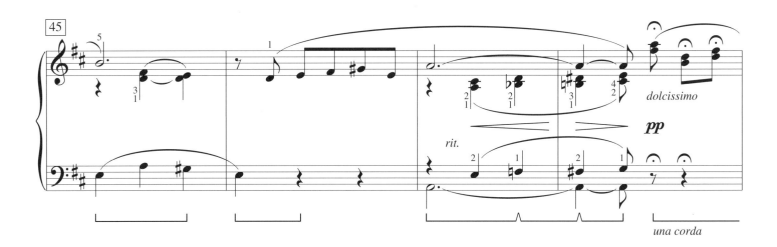

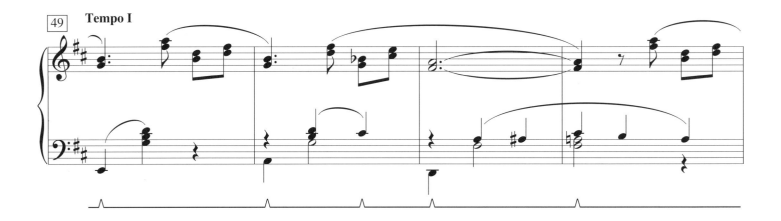

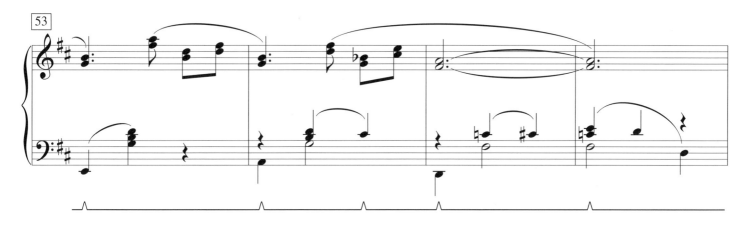

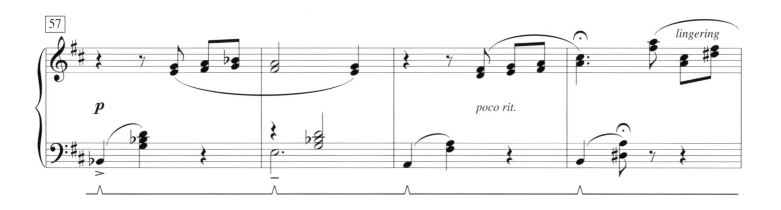

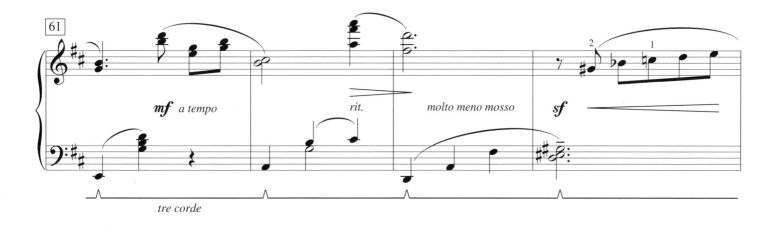

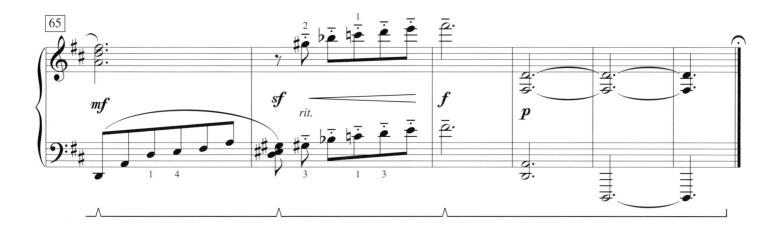

Valse Etude

Especially for Student Affiliate of Dallas Music Teachers' Association

William Gillock

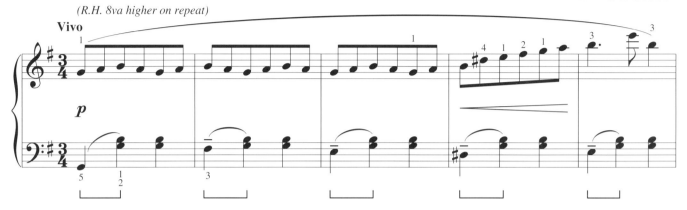

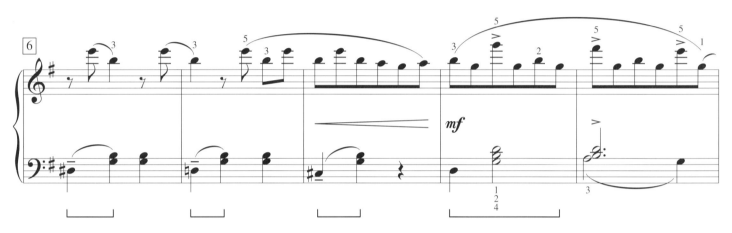

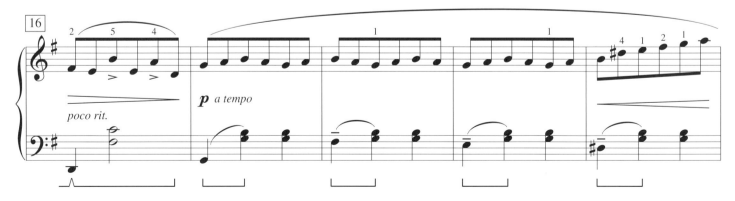

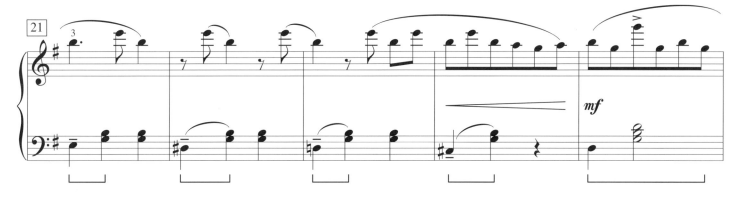

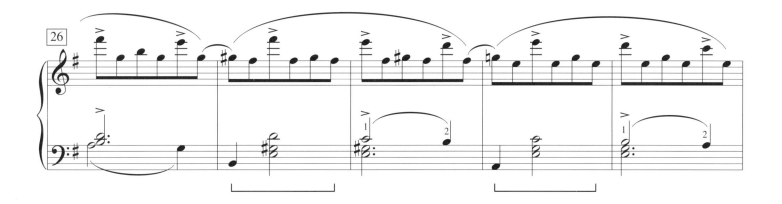

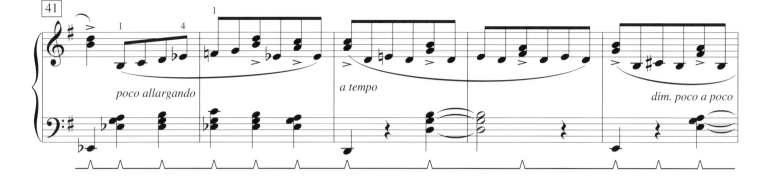

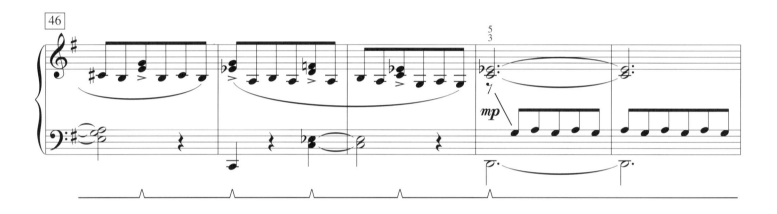

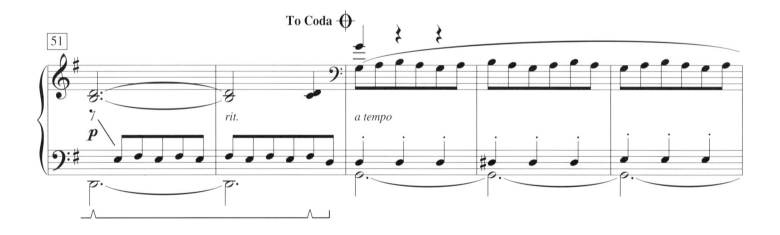

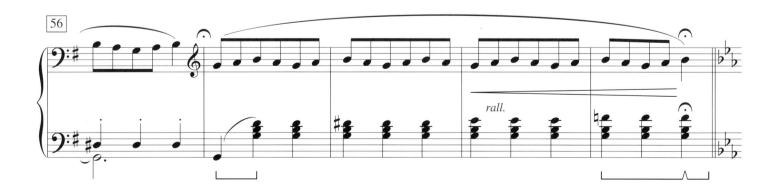

Meno mosso e molto lirico

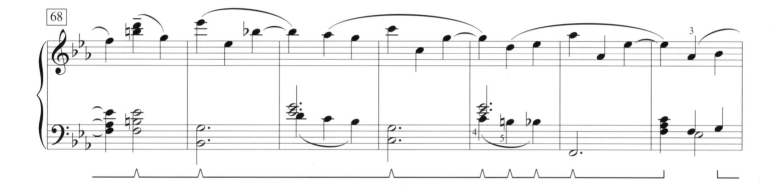

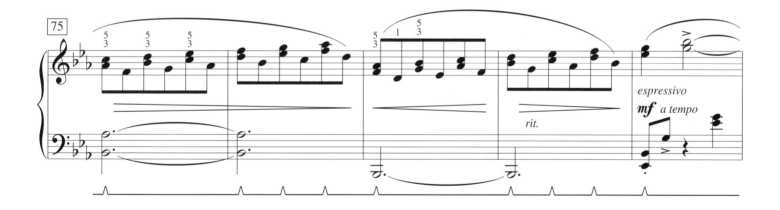

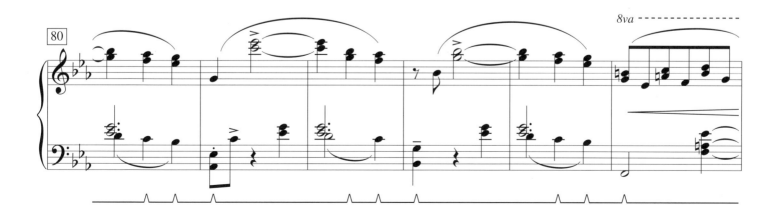

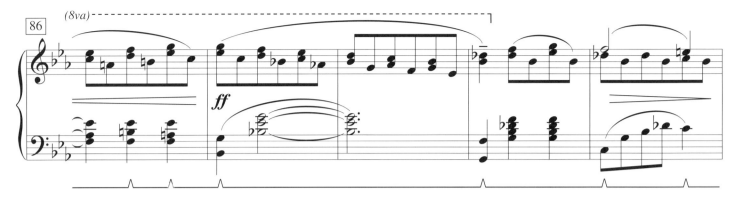

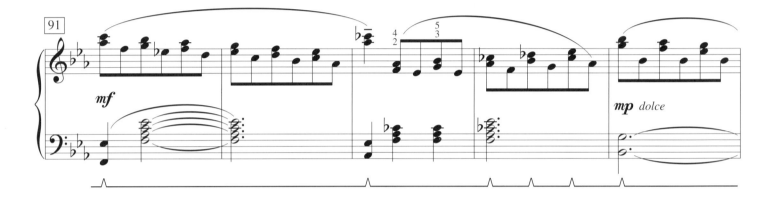

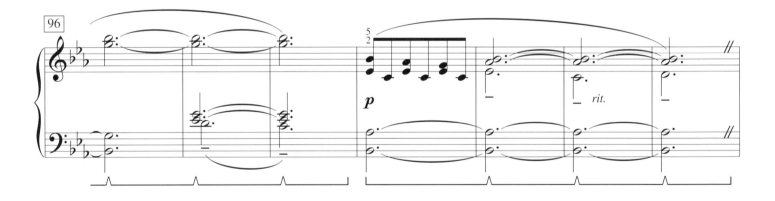

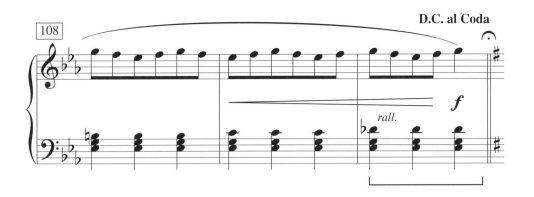
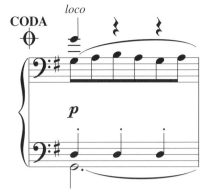

D.C. al Coda

CODA

loco

rall.

f

p

mf

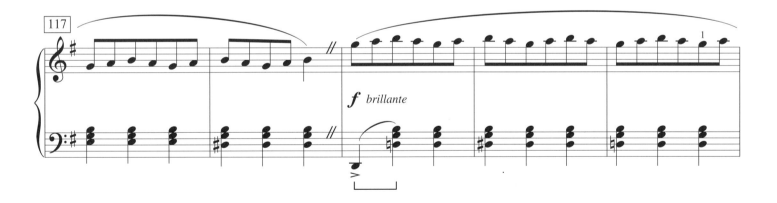

f brillante

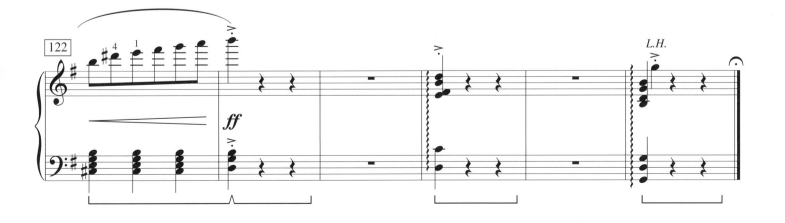

ff

L.H.

To George Kelver

Sonatine

William Gillock

I. Moderately fast (♩ = ca. 132)

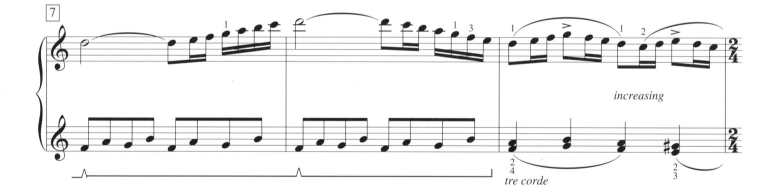

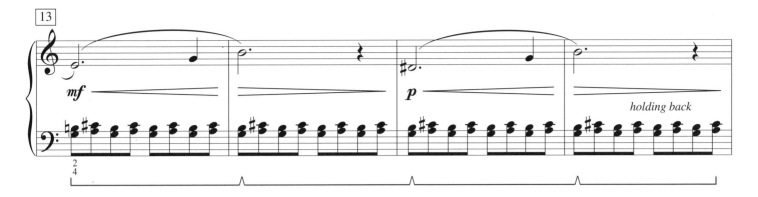

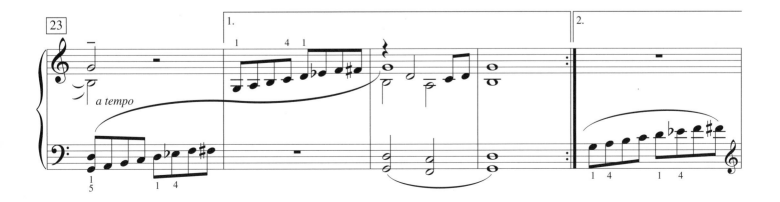

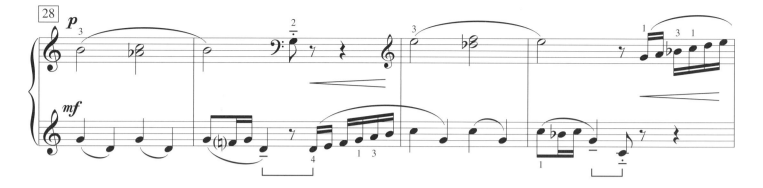

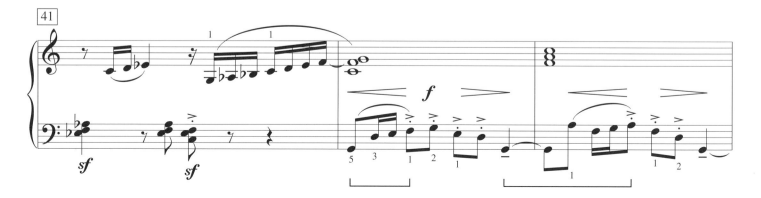

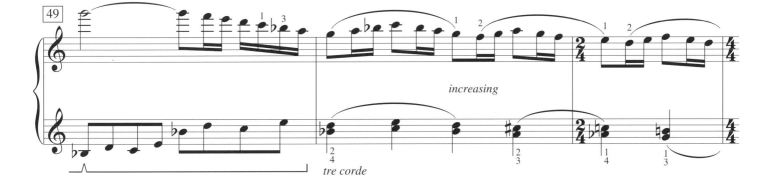

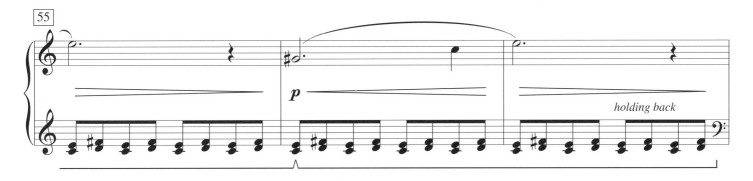

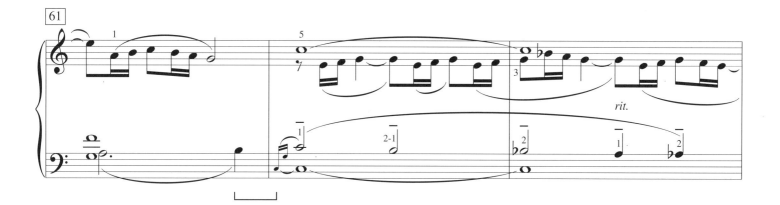

II. Slowly, with drowsy movement (♪ = ca. 116)

una corda

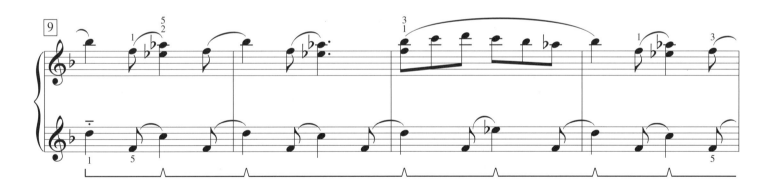

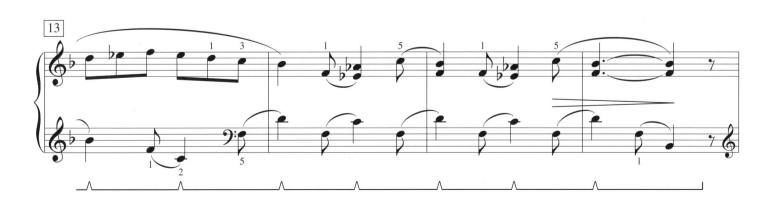

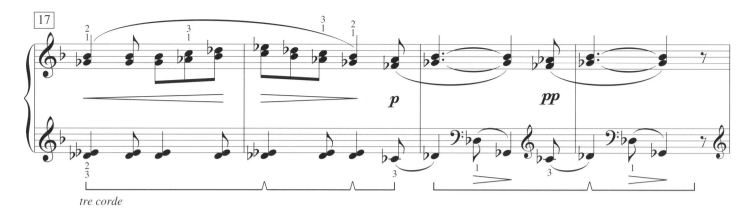

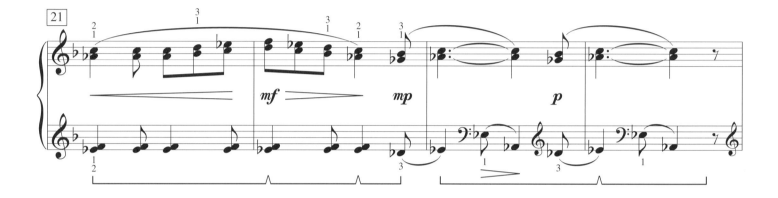

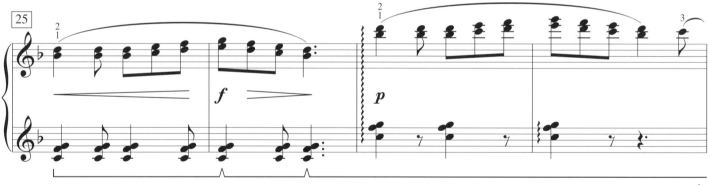

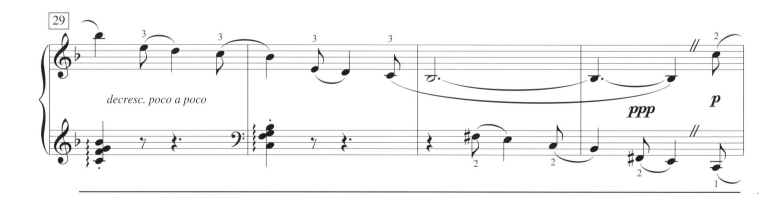

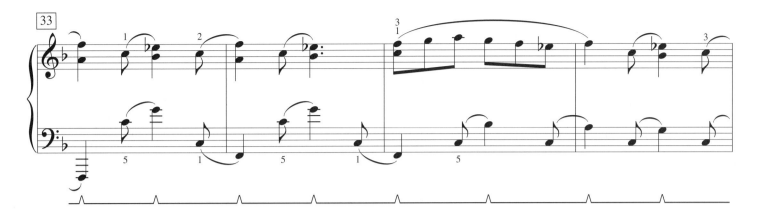

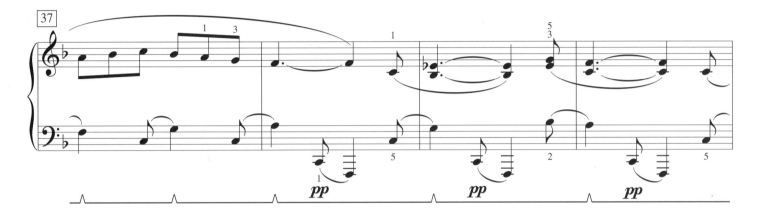

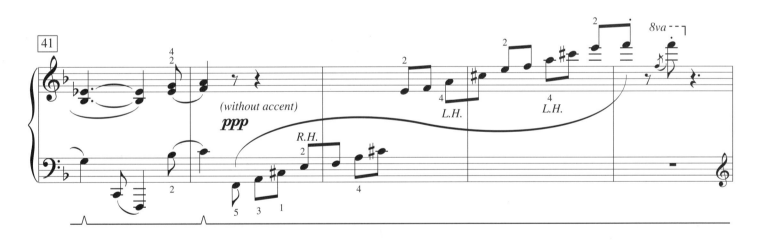

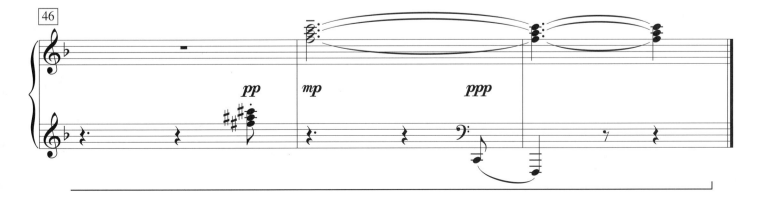

III. Rondo; vigorously, rhythmically (♩ = ca. 138)

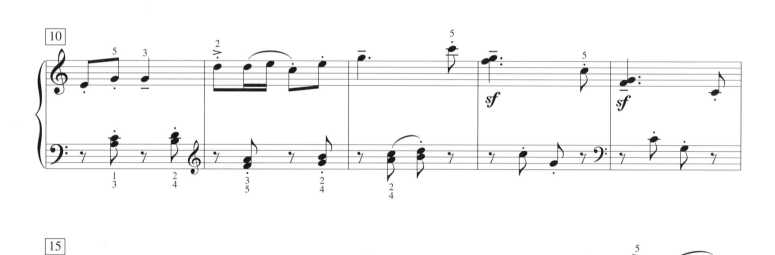

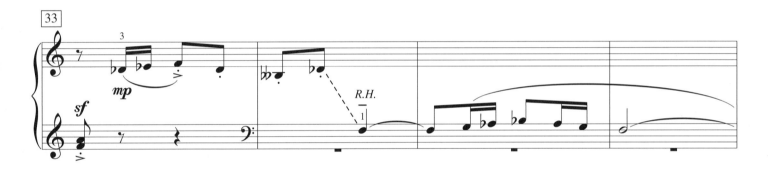

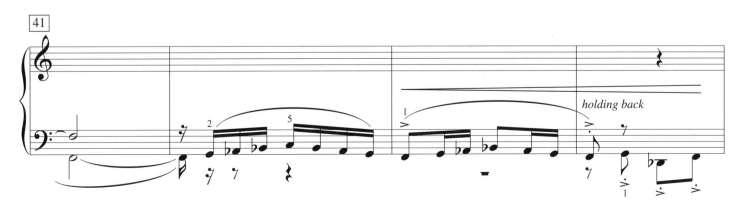

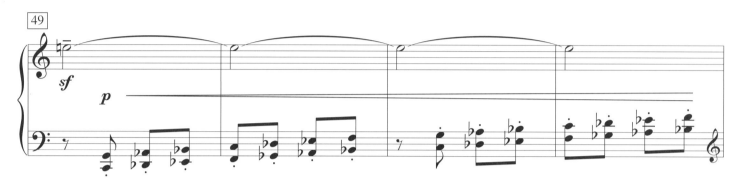

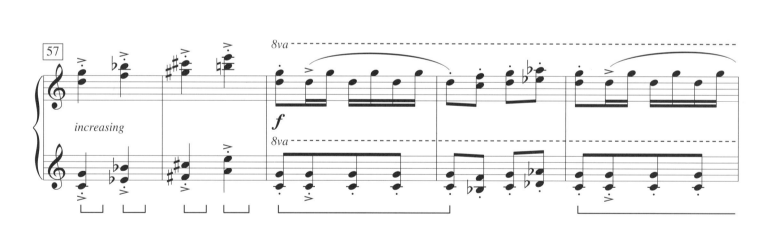

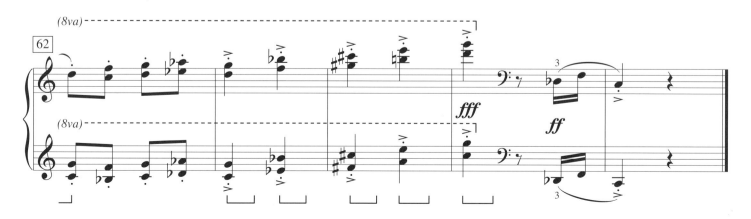

Spectacular Piano Solos

from

WILLIS MUSIC

www.willispianomusic.com

Early Elementary

00416850	Barnyard Strut/*Glenda Austin*	$2.99
00416702	Big Green Frog/*Carolyn C. Setliff*	$2.99
00416904	The Blizzard/*Glenda Austin*	$2.99
00416882	Bow-Wow Blues/*Glenda Austin*	$2.99
00406670	Cookies/*Carolyn Miller*	$2.99
00404218	Fog at Sea/*William Gillock*	$2.99
00416907	Guardian Angels/*Naoko Ikeda*	$3.99
00416918	Halloween Surprise/*Ronald Bennett*	$2.99
00412099	Moccasin Dance/*John Thompson*	$2.99
00416783	My Missing Teeth/*Carolyn C. Setliff*	$2.95
00416933	The Perceptive Detective/*Carolyn Miller*	$2.99
00416816	Rain, Rain/*Carolyn Miller*	$2.99

Mid-Elementary

00416780	The Acrobat/*Carolyn Miller*	$2.99
00416041	Autumn Is Here/*William Gillock*	$3.99
00416803	The Dancing Bears/*Carolyn Miller*	$2.99
00416878	Mini Toccata/*Eric Baumgartner*	$2.99
00416958	Miss Kitty Kat/*Glenda Austin*	$2.99
00404738	Moonlight/*William Gillock*	$3.99
00416872	The Rainbow/*Carolyn Miller*	$2.99
00416728	Seahorse Serenade/*Carolyn C. Setliff*	$2.95
00416674	Seaside Dancer/*Ronald Bennett*	$2.50

Later Elementary

00416852	Black Cat Chat/*Eric Baumgartner*	$2.99
00416786	Egyptian Journey/*Randall Hartsell*	$2.95
00416906	Evening Melody/*Naoko Ikeda*	$3.99
00416886	Flying Fingers/*Carolyn C. Setliff*	$3.99
00416836	The Gentle Brook/*Carolyn Miller*	$2.99
00416908	The Goblins Gather/*Frank Levin*	$2.99
00405918	Monkey on a Stick/*Lynn Freeman Olson*	$2.95
00416866	October Leaves/*Carolyn C. Setliff*	$2.99
00406552	Parisian Waltz/*Robert Donahue*	$2.95
00416781	The Race Car/*Carolyn Miller*	$2.99
00406564	Showdown/*Ronald Bennett*	$2.99
00416919	Sparkling Waterfall/*Carolyn C. Setliff*	$2.99
00416820	Star Wonders/*Randall Hartsell*	$2.99
00416779	Sunrise at San Miguel/*Ronald Bennett*	$3.99
00416881	Twilight Tarantella/*Glenda Austin*	$2.99

Early Intermediate

00416943	Autumn Nocturne/*Susan Alcon*	$2.99
00405455	Bass Train Boogie/*Stephen Adoff*	$2.99
00416817	Broken Arm Blues/*Carolyn Miller*	$2.99
00416841	The Bubbling Brook/*Carolyn Miller*	$2.99
00416849	Bye-Bye Blues/*Glenda Austin*	$2.99
00416945	Cafe Francais/*Jonathan Maiocco*	$2.99
00416834	Canopy of Stars/*Randall Hartsell*	$2.99
00416956	Dancing in a Dream/*William Gillock*	$3.99
00415585	Flamenco/*William Gillock*	$2.99
00416856	Garden of Dreams/*Naoko Ikeda*	$2.99
00416818	Majestic Splendor/*Carolyn C. Setliff*	$2.99
00416948	Manhattan Swing/*Naoko Ikeda*	$2.99
00416733	The Matador/*Carolyn Miller*	$3.99

00416940	Medieval Rondo/*Carolyn C. Setliff*	$2.99
00416942	A Melancholy Night/*Naoko Ikeda*	$3.99
00416877	Mystic Quest/*Randall Hartsell*	$2.99
00416873	Le Papillon (The Butterfly)/*Glenda Austin*	$2.99
00416829	Scherzo Nuovo/*Eric Baumgartner*	$2.99
00416947	Snowflakes in Spring/*Naoko Ikeda*	$2.99
00416937	Stampede/*Carolyn Miller*	$2.99
00416917	Supernova/*Ronald Bennett*	$2.99
00416842	Tarantella in G Minor/*Glenda Austin*	$3.99
00416782	Toccata Caprice/*Carolyn C. Setliff*	$2.95
00416938	Toccatina Tag/*Ronald Bennett*	$2.99
00416869	Twilight Tapestry/*Randall Hartsell*	$2.99
00416924	A Waltz to Remember/*Glenda Austin*	$3.99

Mid-Intermediate

00416911	Blues Streak/*Eric Baumgartner*	$2.99
00416855	Dance of the Unicorn/*Naoko Ikeda*	$2.99
00416893	Fantasia in A Minor/*Randall Hartsell*	$2.99
00416821	Foggy Blues/*Naoko Ikeda*	$3.99
00414908	Fountain in the Rain/*William Gillock*	$3.99
00416765	Grand Sonatina in G/*Glenda Austin*	$2.95
00416875	Himalayan Grandeur/*Randall Hartsell*	$2.99
00406630	Jazz Suite No. 2/*Glenda Austin*	$4.99
00416910	Little Rock (& Roll)/*Eric Baumgartner*	$3.99
00416939	Midnight Fantasy/*Carolyn C. Setliff*	$2.99
00416857	Moonlight Rose/*Naoko Ikeda*	$2.99
00414627	Portrait of Paris/*William Gillock*	$2.99
00405171	Sea Nocturne/*Glenda Austin*	$2.99
00416844	Sea Tempest/*Randall Hartsell*	$2.99
00415517	Sonatine/*William Gillock*	$4.99
00416701	Spanish Romance/*arr. Frank Levin*	$2.95
00416946	Stormy Seas/*Carolyn Miller*	$3.99
00416100	Three Jazz Preludes/*William Gillock*	$4.99

Later Intermediate

00416764	Romantic Rhapsody/*Glenda Austin*	$4.99
00405646	Soft Lights/*Carolyn Jones Campbell*	$2.99
00409464	Tarantella/*A. Pieczonka*	$3.99

Early Advanced

00415263	Impromptu/*Mildred T. Souers*	$2.99
00415166	Sleighbells in the Snow/*William Gillock*	$4.99
00405264	Valse Brillante/*Glenda Austin*	$4.99

HAL•LEONARD® CORPORATION

7777 W. BLUEMOUND RD. P.O. BOX 13819 MILWAUKEE, WI 53213

CLOSER LOOK View sample pages and hear audio excerpts online at **www.halleonard.com**

www.facebook.com/willispianomusic

0322
357

MUSIC FROM

William Gillock
Available exclusively from Willis Music

"The Gillock name spells magic to teachers around the world..."
Lynn Freeman Olson, renowned piano pedagogue

NEW ORLEANS JAZZ STYLES

William Gillock's bestselling *New Orleans Jazz Styles* have been repertoire staples since the 1960s. He believed that every student's musical education should include experiences in a variety of popular styles, including jazz, as a recurring phase of study. Because spontaneity is an essential ingredient of the jazz idiom, performers are encouraged to incorporate their own improvisations.

NEW ORLEANS JAZZ STYLES
Mid-Intermediate
New Orleans Nightfall • The Constant Bass • Mardi Gras • Dixieland Combo • Frankie and Johnny (Theme and Variations).
00415931 Book Only $6.99

MORE NEW ORLEANS JAZZ STYLES
Mid-Intermediate
New Orleans Blues • Taking It Easy • After Midnight • Mister Trumpet Man • Bourbon Street Saturday Night.
00415946 Book Only............... $6.99

STILL MORE NEW ORLEANS JAZZ STYLES
Mid-Intermediate
Mississippi Mud • Uptown Blues • Downtown Beat • Canal Street Blues • Bill Bailey.
00404401 Book Only............... $6.99

NEW ORLEANS JAZZ STYLES – COMPLETE EDITION
Mid to Late Intermediate
This complete collection features updated engravings for all 15 original piano solos. In addition, access to orchestrated online audio files is provided.
00416922 Book/Online Audio... $19.99

NEW ORLEANS JAZZ STYLES DUETS – COMPLETE EDITION
Early to Mid-Intermediate
arr. Glenda Austin
All 15 pieces from Gillock's classic *New Orleans Jazz Styles* series adapted for piano duet! Includes access to audio files online for practice.
00362327 Book/Online Audio .. $14.99

NEW ORLEANS JAZZ STYLES SIMPLIFIED – COMPLETE EDITION
Late Elementary to Early Intermediate
arr. Glenda Austin
All 15 songs from the *New Orleans Jazz Styles* series adapted for easy piano.
00357095 3 Books in One!....... $12.99

ACCENT ON... SERIES

ACCENT ON GILLOCK SERIES
Excellent piano solos for recitals in all levels by Gillock.

$5.99 each
00405993 Volume 1
00405994 Volume 2
00405995 Volume 3
00405996 Volume 4

$6.99 each
00405997 Volume 5
00405999 Volume 6
00406000 Volume 7
00406001 Volume 8

Complete Edition
00361225 8 Books in One! $24.99

ACCENT ON... REPERTOIRE BOOKS

00415712	**Analytical Sonatinas** Early Intermediate......$7.99
00122148	**Around the World** Early Intermediate........ $8.99
00415797	**Black Keys** Mid-Intermediate.................. $5.99
00416932	**Classical** Early to Mid-Intermediate........... $8.99
00415748	**Majors** Late Elementary....................... $6.99
00415569	**Majors & Minors** Early Intermediate.........$7.99
00415165	**Rhythm & Style** Mid-Intermediate............ $6.99
00118900	**Seasons** Early Intermediate.................... $8.99
00278505	**Timeless Songs** Early Intermediate......... $12.99

ACCENT ON DUETS
Mid to Later Intermediate
8 original duets, including: Sidewalk Cafe • Liebesfreud (Kreisler) • Jazz Prelude • Dance of the Sugar Plum Fairy (Tchaikovsky) • Fiesta Mariachi.
00416804 1 Piano/4 Hands $13.99

ACCENT ON SOLOS – COMPLETE
Early to Late Elementary
All 3 of Gillock's popular *Accent on Solos* books. These 33 short teaching pieces continue to motivate piano students of every age!
00200896...........................$14.99

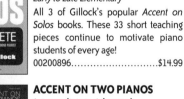

ACCENT ON TWO PIANOS
Intermediate to Advanced
Titles: Carnival in Rio • On a Paris Boulevard • Portrait of Paris • Viennese Rondo. Includes a duplicate score insert for the second piano.
00146176 2 Pianos, 4 Hands..... $12.99

ALSO AVAILABLE

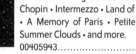

CLASSIC PIANO REPERTOIRE – WILLIAM GILLOCK
Elementary
8 great solos have been re-engraved for this collection: Little Flower Girl of Paris • Spooky Footsteps • On a Paris Boulevard • Stately Sarabande • Rocking Chair Blues • and more!
00416957.............................$8.99

CLASSIC PIANO REPERTOIRE – WILLIAM GILLOCK
Intermediate to Advanced
A dozen delightful pieces have been re-engraved in this collection. Includes favorites such as *Valse Etude, Festive Piece, Polynesian Nocturne*, and *Sonatine*.
00416912............................$12.99

LYRIC PIECES
Early Intermediate
Most of these wonderfully warm and lyrical short pieces are one-page long. Includes: Drifting Clouds • Homage to Chopin • Intermezzo • Land of Pharaoh • A Memory of Paris • Petite Etude • Summer Clouds • and more.
00405943............................ $7.99

WILLIAM GILLOCK RECITAL COLLECTION
Intermediate to Advanced
Features an extensive compilation of over 50 of William Gillock's most popular and frequently performed recital pieces. Newly engraved and edited to celebrate Gillock's centennial year.
00201747...$19.99

A YOUNG PIANIST'S FIRST BIG NOTE SOLOS
Early to Mid-Intermediate
10 short solos perfect for a student's first recital: Clowns • Glass Slipper • Let's Waltz • The Little Shepherd • New Roller Skates • Pagoda Bells • Smoke Signals • Spooky Footsteps • Swing Your Partner • Water Lilies.
00416229..................................... $6.99

*Many more collections, duets and solo sheets available by William Gillock. Search for these and more Willis Music publications for piano at **willispianomusic.com**.*

Find us online at
willispianomusic.com

WILLIS MUSIC

EXCLUSIVELY DISTRIBUTED BY
HAL•LEONARD®

1220
381